Laura's Guide to Buying the Perfect Home in Greater Daytona Beach

Laura's Guide to Buying the Perfect Home in Greater Daytona Beach

Laura Edwards

iUniverse, Inc.
New York Lincoln Shanghai

Laura's Guide to Buying the Perfect Home in Greater Daytona Beach

iUniverse books may be ordered through booksellers or by contacting:

iUniverse
2021 Pine Lake Road, Suite 100
Lincoln, NE 68512
www.iuniverse.com
1-800-Authors (1-800-288-4677)

ISBN-13: 978-0-595-37255-3 (pbk)
ISBN-13: 978-0-595-81652-1 (ebk)
ISBN-10: 0-595-37255-4 (pbk)
ISBN-10: 0-595-81652-5 (ebk)

Printed in the United States of America

Contents

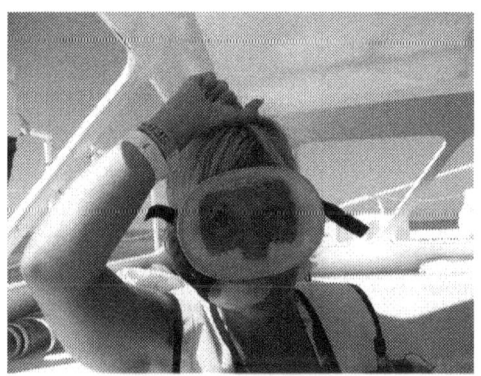

Ready to Go?
Let's Dive In...

Introduction

Why Daytona?

Known as "The World's Most Famous Beach", Daytona Beach and the surrounding areas offer great weather, soft sandy beaches, and lots of wonderful activities. Whether you like fishing, racing, boating, surfing, golfing, tennis, skydiving, or great dining and dancing, it's all here, year round. It's the home of NASCAR, Hawaiian Tropic, the Ladies Professional Golf Association (LPGA), the world's largest Harley-Davidson dealership, and the Florida home of the United States Tennis Association (USTA). Daytona sits on the Atlantic coast at the north end of the "I-4 corridor" which stretches south-west through Orlando, to Tampa. This corridor is one of Florida's fastest growing commercial zones, attracting dozens of new high tech companies each year. The greater Daytona area encompasses Daytona Beach and the surrounding cities, which stretch along the east coast of Volusia County. Each of these cities has much to offer those looking to find their place in the sun. Some might argue that greater Daytona extends as far north as Palm Coast, and as far west as DeLand.

As commerce grows northward from Orlando toward Daytona, job opportunities expand. Investors realize the greater Daytona Beach area has lots of potential, and unlike South Beach, it's a place where you can still buy property at reasonable prices. Close proximity to Disney World, Sea World, Universal Studios, and the Kennedy Space Center is also attractive. The appeal of bright sunshine and low interest rates makes the area an excellent place to buy investment properties, vacation homes, and retirement homes. Even the threat of hurricanes hasn't dampened the desire to own property here. While home prices continue to rise, homes in the area are a bargain, and an excellent investment compared to other parts of Florida and the U.S.

My Background

I was born and raised in Ormond Beach, the youngest of 7 children and soon after graduation from Seabreeze High School, I moved to Seattle, Washington. Shortly thereafter, I began my real estate career with Century 21, one of the most recognized and trusted names in the industry. Selling real estate in Seattle, along the shores of Puget Sound, was a wonderful experience, but after twelve years in the Seattle area, I decided to return home to Ormond Beach. Although Seattle is a beautiful city, the moderate temperatures and sunny days were something I always missed. I again went to work for Century 21, this time with A.H. Stone & Associates, Inc., also in Ormond Beach. Over the years I've helped hundreds of people buy and sell their homes, always putting their best interests above all else. I've taken great care to manage my clients' transactions in an honest, professional manner, while paying close attention to detail and providing the quality service expected of a Century 21 Realtor®.

Just as I've watched the Daytona area change over the years, I've also watched the business of Real Estate change dramatically since I first began my career—does anyone remember dot-matrix printers and bag-phones? My time in Seattle made me realize the importance of staying up-to-date with changes in technology. As such, I was one of the first Realtors®in the Daytona Beach area with a personal website, http://greaterdaytona.com. This website has made it possible for me to attract and serve buyers and investors many miles away, even outside the country. I've sold several homes "sight-unseen" because of today's capability to e-mail digital photos and to handle transactions electronically.

Whether buying their first home, relocating, buying an investment home, or trading up, my customers often face the same hurdles and have the same questions and sometimes even misconceptions about the home buying process. This book is specific to the greater Daytona Beach area, and provides valuable information on how to find and buy the home you really want, in a market where competition for homes remains strong.

Views of Downtown Daytona Beach

Chapter 1

All About Realtors®

I begin with this topic because many buyers don't understand what Realtors® do, and why it's important to work with one. Also confusing is the role of brokers and the Multiple Listing Service.

Realtors® are an important part of the home buying process. Besides finding homes for our customers, we perform many behind-the-scenes activities that many home buyers have little experience with. In fact, finding the right home is just the beginning of the process. The functions we perform after a contract is written are what make us most valuable. We help negotiate with the seller, schedule the inspections and appraisal, coordinate repairs if needed, and work with the lender and title company to ensure the process is as smooth as possible.

Why Use a Realtor®?

- **We Know the Market**

We know the area and the local real estate market. We know what's hot and what's not. We know how to find the kind of home you'll be comfortable with and can advise you on what is a good investment, and what isn't.

- **We're Professionals**

We abide by a professional code of ethics, which means we not only do what's legal, we do what's right. We keep you informed and return your phone calls. Reputation means everything so we work hard for you.

- **We Use Technology to Serve You Better**

We use e-mail, the Internet, and our personal websites to provide our customers with up-to-date, accurate information. Technology allows us to work with customers around the world and to stay in close contact with sellers, lenders and others.

- **Representation**

Although most of us are not attorneys, we are trained in Real Estate Law. We can prepare and present your offer to the seller, provide assistance with counter-offers and contingencies, and make sure the seller provides the proper disclosures. We're available for inspections and appraisals and work to keep things moving smoothly. We are here for you and look out for your best interests.

- **We Know the Process**

We're experienced in working with lenders, title companies, appraisers, inspectors, buyers, sellers, and other Agents. Upon your request, we can suggest alternate lenders that will work with your situation. We can also recommend local companies you can depend on, whether you need a mortgage or a moving company.

- **Our Services are Free to the Buyer**

Typically, when dealing with residential real estate, realty fees are a charge to the seller. The seller offers a commission to cooperating agents in exchange for them showing their home and procuring a buyer. This means that all of the training, services, experience, and expertise of a Real Estate Agent can be yours for free.

Finding a Realtor®

The terms "Realtors®," "Real Estate Agents," and "Agents," are used interchangeably but there is a difference. Realtors® must belong to the "National Association of Realtors®" and are bound by the association's Code of Ethics. As members, Realtors® have access to the local MLS, continuing education, and up-to-date information on the local real estate market.

If you don't know a good Realtor®, ask your friends and family, look in local real estate publications or the Sunday paper. If you have Internet access, do a search for "Daytona Beach Real Estate" and check out some of the real estate web sites that come up. Feel free to interview several Agents and ask for references. You don't need the "Top Producer," just someone you feel has the knowledge, experience, and character needed to assist you and answer your questions along the way. Your Agent will be your partner throughout the entire process, keeping your information confidential, and looking out for your best interests at all times. Your Agent is also required to tell you any information known about the properties you're interested in, including future land use and planning issues.

Brokers

Realtors® work under the guidance of a "Broker." A Broker has special training and licenses, which allow him/her to manage a real estate office. In most cases, the Broker provides office space and pays for franchise fees, utilities, fax machines, computers, advertising, and other office expenses. A Broker usually has several Agents working under him/her.

Realtors®

While the Broker manages the office and provides support, the Realtors® are the ones most often dealing directly with buyers and sellers. Each Realtor® operates as an independent contractor. We pay income taxes quarterly, and are responsible for our own healthcare and retirement planning. Other expenses include the cost of advertising our listings, personal promotion, continuing education, annual dues, cell phone service, Internet service, personal websites, home office equipment, supplies, and lots of gas, tires, and oil.

The Local Board of Realtors®

Geographic areas are divided into local "Boards." Each Board represents its members and provides services, education, and a local MLS system. Brokers and Realtors® often join multiple Boards in order to have access to each Board's MLS.

Real Estate Fees (commissions)

The real estate fee or commission, is usually a percentage of the sales price, and is negotiated when a home is listed for sale. When the transaction successfully closes, and only if it closes, the fee is paid. In return for this fee, the seller's home is marketed through the MLS, real estate publications, newspapers, the Internet, and numerous other sources. The Listing Agent may also provide "virtual tours" and other services, such as assistance "staging" the home so it will be more appealing to prospective buyers. With the seller's permission, the Listing Agent will also place a For Sale sign in the yard, put a lock box on the door, prepare flyers, and hold an Open House one or more times to further market the home. The Listing Agent will also show the home to prospective buyers and will look out for the interests of the seller. All of theses services are provided at the Listing Agent's expense whether the home sells or not.

How is The Commission Paid?

The commission is most often split into two "sides." This is because in most cases, a home listed with an Agent in one office (listing side) is sold by an Agent from another office (selling side.) Each office gets one side of the commission. In the event the Listing Agent sells the home, the full commission will go to the listing office.

What is The MLS?

When a home is "listed" for sale through a realty company that's a member of the National Association or Realtors® (some realty companies aren't members), the listing is entered into a real estate database called the Multiple Listing Service (MLS). Besides current listings, the MLS contains a wealth of information about past sales, property taxes, school districts, and more. Listings in the MLS can be viewed via the Internet through a variety of real estate websites, and many Agents, also provide access to MLS listings through their own personal web sites as I do.

Why do you need a Realtor® when you have the Internet?

Besides the reasons just mentioned, house hunting on the Internet is time consuming. While the Internet is a good place to find information and get a feel for what homes are selling for, it can't do everything for you. Once you find a listing you're interested in, you'll probably want to see the inside before making an offer. If you're a local buyer, an Agent can let you in. If you're from another state or another country, an Agent can evaluate the home for you, and e-mail digital photos. Later, I will explain how to effectively use the Internet when hunting for a home.

NOTE: Real Estate Agents can show you ANY home listed with ANY realty company, not just those listed with their own company. There are few exceptions. In fact, a licensed Florida Realtor® can sell homes anywhere in Florida. They can also refer you to reputable Agents whether you're moving across the state or around the world.

What Not to Do

The Agent you select is going to be working hard for you. For that reason, once you've decided which agent is best for you, you should work exclusively with that person. You have no legal obligation to do so; it's just the right thing to do. If, for example, you see a For Sale sign in front of a nice home, don't call the number on the sign to find out about it, call your Agent. Again, your Agent can open and show you ANY HOME listed for sale. Chances are the home in question is already sold, or is listed for more than you want to spend, or your Agent would have shown it to you already. Trust that your Agent will keep you informed of every available home in your price range.

Maintaining communication is crucial. As noted previously, finding a home is just the beginning of the process, and keeping the transaction from falling apart later can sometimes be difficult. Communication between all parties involved is required to successfully close on a home. Just as you expect us to answer and return your calls, we expect the same of you. We wouldn't call if it weren't important.

Don't play one Agent against another. Since all local Real Estate Agents get their information from the same MLS, don't believe a different Agent will be able to provide a better selection of available homes.

Views of the Halifax Marina

Chapter 2

Financing

Selecting a Lender

A "hot" real estate market is one in which there are more home buyers than there are homes to sell. In other words, demand exceeds supply. While that may sound like a great thing for Real Estate Agents, it's not as great as it would seem. The problem is many people are looking to buy, and the competition is fierce. Sellers may receive several competing offers at the same time, often within one or two days, and homes sell quickly. Whether it's a hot market or not, there will always be competition for homes in a moderate price range, those in the most popular areas, and those with strong investment appeal. For these reasons, it's important for you as a buyer, to make your "highest and best" offer when you find the home you want. A good offer is not just about the money, but having your financing in order is the first important step.

Today there are many places you can go for financing on your new home. There are savings and loan corporations, credit unions, banks, mortgage brokers, and even Internet based lenders available to loan you money. Which one you choose is a personal decision, but what you really want is someone that's easy to reach, and one that's responsive to your needs. You do not want to be on hold for twenty minutes or wade through endless voice menu options to get to a representative. Worse yet is having your call answered by some "help desk trainee." In my experience, local lenders are the most responsive. These lenders also use local appraisers who know and understand the local market. If you don't have a lender in mind, ask friends, relatives, and your Real Estate Agent for recommendations.

Mortgage Brokers

A mortgage broker works with multiple lenders instead of just one. This flexibility allows them to find the loan that is best for you. Furthermore, if the loan process is started and problems do occur, a mortgage broker can often move your loan to another lender, saving the transaction. The mortgage broker charges a fee for this service, which will be noted on your good faith estimate, and paid at closing.

VA, FHA, and Conventional Loans

The financing you obtain can affect the type and cost of homes you can buy. Government loan programs such as VA, FHA, and others have been extremely beneficial to millions of people but limit how much you can borrow. They also have tighter guidelines concerning the condition of the home and closing costs.

For example, with VA financing, there are closing costs the buyer often cannot pay and which must be paid by the seller. These may include:

- Escrow Fees
- Administrative Fees
- Document Preparation Fees
- Underwriting Review Fees
- Processing Fees
- Wire Fees
- Tax Service Fees
- Notary Fees
- City Transfer Taxes or Tax Stamp Fees

These costs can run into thousands of dollars and may greatly reduce the amount of money the seller ends up with at closing. An offer based on conventional (non-government) financing usually is more appealing to most sellers. In the past, buyers had few options if buying a home with little or no money down, but today, a variety of zero to low money down conventional programs is available.

Other considerations

How much of a down payment or initial investment can you afford? Do you need the seller to help with your closing costs? Do you have a relative willing to give you money to help you buy a home? What are your goals? Do you intend to live in the home for a long time or will you be trading up in a few years. All of these issues should be discussed with your lender in order to determine the loan program that's right for you.

Pre-Qualification

It's pointless to begin looking for homes until you're pre-qualified for a loan, unless of course you won't need financing and you'll be paying cash. In the minds of Real Estate Agents and sellers, you're not a serious buyer unless you have taken this important first step. You don't "fill your shopping cart" and then go off and figure out how to pay for what's in it. The same applies when shopping for a home. The pre-qualification process is free, simple, and can usually be done over the phone, in half an hour or less. It involves contacting a lender and providing basic information about income, debts and expenses. The lender will use ratios such as debt-to-income and debt-to-expenses to determine how much you qualify to borrow. This free service gives a rough estimate of how much the lender is willing to loan towards the purchase of your new home. It will also help determine the price range you should stay within to keep your monthly payments inside your "comfort zone." It's extremely important to be honest, because once you've found the home you want, you'll be asked to provide detailed proof of income before a loan is granted. If you're a singer in a rock band on the weekends, it's ok to claim that income as long as you can prove that you receive it. The point is it's better to be honest with the lender. Otherwise you may be pre-qualified for more than you can really borrow. You don't want to make an offer on the perfect house, only to find the lender won't loan you the money to buy it. It's embarrassing and costly to back out of a deal, and frustrating to start house hunting all over again.

Call several lenders, because each one is different. I once worked with a frustrated family who after weeks of looking couldn't find a suitable home in their price range. At my suggestion, they called another lender and were pre-qualified for significantly more money. This one phone call was all it took to turn them into homeowners. When comparing lenders, be sure to ask about administrative, processing, and other fees which can add significantly to the cost of the loan.

Lenders offering the lowest interest rates may also charge the highest fees. Ask a lot of questions so there are no surprises at the closing table.

Once pre-qualified, your lender will fax a "pre-qual" letter stating the amount you're pre-qualified for, to you and/or your Agent. This letter may be submitted along with your offer when you're ready to buy.

How Much Money Do You Need to Buy A House?

Even if you qualify for a "no money down" loan, you'll need money for many of the following items:

* **Good Faith Deposit**

A good faith deposit, also called a "binder", "earnest money" or "escrow," is just another term for deposit. When you find the home you want and are ready to make an offer, you'll be expected to put down some money as proof you're serious about buying the house. In effect, you're asking the seller to accept your offer over all others, and take the house off the market. To the seller, the size of the deposit reflects how serious you really are. A check for one to two percent of the purchase price is recommended, but the larger the deposit, the more seriously your offer will be considered. A seller who questions your sincerity may also ask that you increase your deposit. The deposit check is usually placed in a non interest-bearing escrow account maintained by the company your Agent works for (Century 21, etc.), or can be held by a title company or an attorney. It's important to realize that if your offer is accepted, the deposit is between you and the seller. This means that only the seller can release your deposit in the event you don't follow through with the purchase. This deposit therefore serves two purposes. It proves you're serious about buying the house, and serves as compensation to the seller if you later change your mind for the wrong reasons. In other words, this money is refundable depending on how your offer is written, but it is possible to lose it. At closing, your good faith deposit will be counted as part of your down payment.

* **Down payment**

The down payment is the amount the lender requires you to contribute toward the purchase of your new home. This amount should have been discussed during the pre-qualification process. Amounts vary widely but typically you can expect to put down a minimum of 3-5% of the purchase price. If you are purchasing the home for investment purposes only, most lenders will require 10-20% or more. The final amount needed depends on your credit worthiness and financial situation.

• Inspections

It's always wise to get a home and pest inspection, even if you are purchasing the home "as-is". Often lenders will require a "clear" pest inspection as a condition of granting your loan. If there's a septic tank involved, or other issues such as wetlands or lead paint, additional inspections may be desired. Expect to spend $300-$500 for home and pest inspections depending on the size of the home. Some companies will do a combined home and pest inspection, possibly saving you a little money. Inspections are your responsibility and must be paid for the day the inspection is performed. It's always a good idea to be present at the inspection so you can discuss any concerns you have with the inspector and have him/her point out any issues or problems.

• Appraisal

Unless you're making a very large down payment, your lender will require a professional appraisal of the homes value. The appraisal is confirmation that the home is worth the purchase price. The lender will ask for, or "order" the appraisal at your expense, and the money is usually collected when you apply for your loan. You can expect to pay $300 or more for the appraisal depending on the size of the home.

• Homeowner's Insurance

The lender will require that you purchase insurance on the home they are financing. You can expect to spend $500–$1,000 or more on insurance, and the policy must be purchased before closing day. If the home is in a flood zone, additional insurance is required.

• Loan Application Fee

Once you've made an offer on a home and are ready to proceed with financing, most lenders will charge a fee to process your loan application. This fee is usually paid up-front, and you can expect to pay $250 or more. Some lenders will apply these funds towards your closing costs.

•   Example of Up-front Expenses

For a $250,000 home purchase, you can roughly expect the following out-of-pocket expenses before closing:

Good Faith Deposit (1%)	$2,500
Loan Application Fee	$ 250
Home Inspection	$ 300
Pest Inspection	$ 75
Appraisal	$ 300
Insurance	$ 800
Total	$4,225

The down payment and other expenses, called "settlement costs" or "closing costs," will be due at closing (the day you actually sign the paperwork and take possession of the home). These may include fees for:

- Property Survey
- Elevation Study (if in a flood zone)
- Loan Origination
- Credit Report
- Assessments
- Abstract or Title Search
- Title Insurance
- Document Preparation
- Recording Fees
- Doc Stamps
- Property Taxes
- Administrative/Processing Fees

Some of these costs may be bundled into the home loan, and others you pay on the spot, along with your down payment. A summary of these costs should be provided by your lender in the form of a "Good Faith Estimate" within three days of applying for the loan.

•   Monthly Payment—Principal, Interest, Taxes & Insurance (PITI) & PMI

Monthly payments are determined by adding together the cost of the loan (principal and interest), the property taxes, homeowner's insurance and

Private Mortgage Insurance (PMI). PMI is a type of insurance required by many lenders whenever the down payment is less than 20% of the value of the home. This insurance protects the lender when a buyer defaults on a loan. Rates vary by the type of loan and the amount of the down payment but in general, it's about ½ of 1 percent. Once you've achieved 20% equity in your home, either through payments or through appreciation of the home's value, you should request that PMI be dropped from your monthly payment. Property taxes are another expense that must be considered. If you're going to live in the home, you'll want to apply for the homestead exemption which reduces the amount you're taxed on by $25,000. For a true estimate of the tax expense on a particular home, I recommend calling the Volusia County Property Appraiser's Office. Finally, there's the monthly cost of homeowner's insurance. While taxes and insurance are only paid once a year, a portion is usually collected by the mortgage company each month so funds will be available when the bill comes due.

Consider the following example of $150,000 home purchased with 2.5% down, an interest rate of 6%, and a loan period of 30 years:

Purchase Price	$150,000.00
Down Payment 2.5%	-$3,750.00
Amount Financed	$146,250.00
Costs per Month	
Principal & Interest(loan payment)	876.84
Private Mortgage Insurance (.005%)	60.94
Homeowners Insurance(~$800 per year)	83.33
Property Taxes (estimate)	242.83
Total Monthly Pmt	**1,263.95**

While interest and property taxes add to the cost of owning a home, a portion of these items is deductible from your personal income tax, off-setting some of the expense. While you're making your monthly payments, the value of your home will continue to rise (appreciate) as well. Using the figures above and assuming a personal income tax rate of 15%, and a modest appreciation rate of only two percent, the following comparison illustrates the advantage of owning a home over renting one.

Cost To Rent

First, Last, Security	3,750.00
Monthly Rent	1,250.00
Annual Cost to Rent	**15,000.00**
Home Equity Appreciation	.00
Tax deductions	.00
Total Benefit	**.00**

Cost to Own

Purchase Price	150,000.00
Down Payment (2.5%)	-3,750.00
Amount Financed	146,250.00
Monthly Payment	**1,263.95**
Annual Cost to Own	**15,167.36**
Home Equity Appreciation (2%)	3,000.00
Tax Deduction (Mortgage Interest)	1,316.25
Tax Deduction (Property Taxes)	437.10
Total Benefit	**4,753.35**

Some or all of the tax deduction may be returned to you when you file your yearly income taxes. The appreciation is like "money in the bank" that will come back to you when you sell your home.

What Not to Do

Let's say you've followed the advice above and have been pre-qualified. You've found a house and made an offer that was accepted by the seller. Maybe the estimated mortgage payment will be less than originally expected so you decide to go furniture shopping or buy a new car. Don't do it! Making a large purchase of any kind could jeopardize your financial position and you could lose the house. The lender is relying on your previously stated income and debts to get the loan approved. A new debt could upset your financial ratios to the point where you no longer qualify. Resist the "urge to splurge" until the home is truly yours.

Are you and your spouse separated, but not yet divorced? If so, don't purchase a home until the divorce is final. While you may qualify on your own, in Florida, your spouse is required to sign the mortgage documents before you can close on a home. This can lead to big problems if your spouse doesn't want to sign. If however, you buy the home as an investment, your spouse does not have to sign. The down side is that investment properties require larger down payments and the interest rates are typically higher too.

Take the time to compare lenders during pre-qualification, and select one before you make an offer on a home. In real estate transactions, time is "of the essence" so don't switch lenders after your offer is accepted. It will slow the process to a crawl, and could cause you to lose the home.

Selected Homes

LPGA
Community in
Daytona Beach

Beachside home
in Daytona
Beach

Ormond Beach home near the Halifax River

Port Orange home in the Oakwater Subdivision

Chapter 3

Finding the Perfect Home

Getting Started

Before you begin your search, consider the needs of your entire household and discuss them with your Agent. What things are most important? Are you looking for something on the beach that suits your active lifestyle or is a certain school district more important? Would you be happy in a condo with no yard or is a ranch home on 10 acres more to your liking? Is an older home suitable or do you prefer new construction? Do you want to live in a gated community or one with few rules and restrictions? How far are you willing to commute to work and/or school? Will you live in the home or rent it out? When will you be available to view homes? Will you be making the final decision on the home purchase or will someone else be involved? Do you prefer to communicate with your Agent using e-mail or the telephone? What's your timeline for moving? Do you have a house to sell before you can buy another? It's important to discuss these issues with your Agent so he/she can better understand your needs.

What's Perfect For You?

- **The Single Family Residence**

Typically, the "American Dream" is a single family home with 3 or more bedrooms, 2 baths and a 2 car garage, and is the most desired type of home on the market. The advantages of owning a single family home include privacy, peace and quiet, your own private yard, and the freedom to customize your home to fit your personal taste. These homes are often easier to sell when it comes time to move on because of their popularity. The disadvantage is that the home owner must maintain the home and lawn, and is responsible for all utilities, repairs and improvements.

- **Townhomes**

Townhomes are also very popular with first time home buyers, investors, retirees, and those looking for a vacation home. Advantages include small yards, patios, balconies and other amenities that give the feel of a single family home but with much less to maintain. Many new developments also include shopping centers and entertainment complexes which provide the convenience and atmosphere of a small town. Often the disadvantage in owning a townhome is that if you want to make changes to the exterior of the property, you may need to follow guidelines set forth by a governing association or you may need to get mutual agreement from your neighbors. Townhomes are attached structures that are owned individually, including the land the structure sits on. There is a maintenance fee associated with townhomes that typically covers insurance on the structure, costs to maintain the grounds, parking lot, entrance sign, outside lighting, pools, tennis courts, clubhouse, exterior of the building, roof, and other common elements.

- **Condominiums**

Condos have grown in popularity in the greater Daytona Beach area throughout the years and are in higher demand than ever before. Oceanfront or Riverfront condos with spectacular views are most desired, however it is possible to find reasonably priced condos within a short driving distance to the beach. Basic cable and water is often included in the condo dues as well. Condos can be an excellent choice, whether to live in or to purchase as an investment. An advantage to owning a condo, especially if you are an out-of-state investor, is that the monthly dues paid to the Association, usually cover insurance, costs to maintain the grounds, parking lot, entrance sign, outside lighting, pools, tennis courts, clubhouses, exterior of the building, roof, pest control, water, sewer and trash. This is of great advantage if you are planning to rent the unit and don't want the worries of upkeep. Be sure to ask about rental restrictions however, as there are often association bylaws governing the length of leasing periods in Condominiums. Resale potential is high also, as there are always retirees and others looking for something with low mainte-nance requirements or who want to be near the water.

What's the difference between a condo and a townhome? The difference is that townhomes always have their entrance on the ground level, and the land is included in the purchase. With a condo, you may have to take the elevator to get to your residence and you don't own the land. Both townhomes and condos require association fees which usually cover insurance on the structure. You may want a separate policy however, to cover personal items such as tele-visions, fixtures, furniture and appliances.

•   Condotels (Condo-hotels)

Also gaining in popularity is the condotel or condo-hotel. Condotels have really "taken off" in recent years, and are highly desired by out-of-state investors. They are basically converted resort hotel rooms or studios, usually on the ocean or river. You purchase the unit, visit when you want, and then have the on-site management company rent the unit out for you when you aren't using it. These are not the same as a time share. You actually own the unit and it's yours when you want to use it. Most also are sold furnished and include a small kitchen which is another plus. This can be an excellent source of income, as the management company sends you a check at the end of each month, for your share of the daily/weekly rentals. You are responsible for the interior of your unit and must pay dues, which most often cover the insurance for the structure, exterior paint, pool, pest control, lawn, common areas, water, sewer, trash and electric. The down side is that lenders typically require 20% down for a purchase and there are strict guidelines for financing, such as shorter loan terms and square footage requirements. The dues can be steep also, so it's wise to ask for financial data, such as rental payment history, as a condition of your offer. Most do not allow you to live in the unit year round or have pets, but there are currently a few that do.

•   Multi-family Dwellings (Duplex-Triplex-Fourplex, etc)

Also popular among savvy investors is the multi-family dwelling. This classifi-cation consists of duplexes, triplexes, fourplexes and greater than five units. The multifamily structure can be an excellent investment, as you typically can purchase the building and maintain a higher cash flow, having multiple ten-ants in the same structure. The down side is that since you own the structure, you will also have to manage the tenants and property yourself or hire an out-side agency to manage things for you. As with other investments, it's important to gather enough financial data, expense history and rental history to allow you to make an informed decision. You'll need to determine what your cash flow will be after expenses, and whether or not it would be a sound investment for you.

• **Vacant Land/Build to Suit**

Buying vacant land and building a custom home is still popular although vacant land anywhere close to the city is increasingly harder to find. Developers have already purchased the most desirable properties for the purpose of building entire developments. The days of buying a vacant lot for $2,000 are over too. Today, a decent lot will cost $60,000 or more. You also have to be careful of environmental concerns and the conservation of wetlands. Add in the high cost of clearing the land, impact fees, building permits, and building materials means building your own is an expensive way to go. If you do want a custom home, it's recommended that you look for available lots in communities where the environmental concerns have already been addressed and where the infrastructure (roads, electricity, water, sewer, etc.) is already in place.

Using the Internet to Find a Home

According to the National Association of Realtors®, over 70% of today's homebuyers begin their home search on the World Wide Web. My web site, http://greaterdaytona.com, offers a free service called "Auto-Update." As new listings are entered into the local MLS, this service compares them against criteria you've defined, then e-mails the appropriate listings to you. Criteria can include location, price, number of bedrooms and bathrooms, and more. It's important to understand that the **local** MLS is updated every day, while **commercial** MLS systems you find on the Internet may be a day or two behind. That's enough time for the perfect house to sell before you even know about it. Because homes in this area are selling quickly, this service can put you ahead of the competition. If you choose to take advantage of Auto-Update, don't limit yourself by being too specific in your criteria. Use a price ceiling slightly higher than you expect to spend and don't restrict yourself to only homes with pools, or in only one area. You may receive listings that are not exactly what you had in mind, but you'll a have better idea of what's available, and what homes are selling for. At the same time, don't be too vague either or you may receive daily e-mails that are 50 pages long.

Use the Internet to research schools, churches, activities, and demographics of the areas you're interested in. Visit mapping websites like Google Maps® and MapQuest® to determine driving distances to work and schools.

Using the Property Appraiser's section of Volusia County Government's website, http://volusia.org, look up property and tax information on listings you receive, as well as recent sales in the neighborhood. If you're interested in foreclosures, you can access public records through the Volusia County Clerk of Courts website, http://clerk.org.

Looking at Homes

Please try to give your Agent advance notice of what you want to see. Most sellers require an appointment, and some require as much as 24 hours notice. Your Agent will try to get you into the homes as quickly as possible, and will schedule appointments at times acceptable to both you and the seller. By planning ahead, your Agent can schedule several appointments for the same day and make the most efficient use of your time.

Newspapers and Other Print Ads

If you're looking in a modest price range, house hunting through the Sunday newspaper and local real estate publications may not be the best way to find a home. Inevitably, you're going to see a home in the paper or a local real estate publication and think your Agent neglected to tell you about it. The truth is many homes sell before they appear in the print ads. This is especially true of homes priced below $200,000. These homes are in high demand by first time homebuyers and investors. As your house-hunting partner, your Agent is going to be giving you up-to-date listing information. If you don't have Internet access or e-mail, your Agent will check the newest listings every day and call when something appropriate comes up. Trust that your Agent is not going to overlook a listing that's perfect for you.

Seeing Potential

Don't be discouraged by what you consider to be bad taste, and don't expect perfection. Every home you enter may have features you don't like, but try to see the home as it could be. Try to imagine it with a fresh coat of paint and your furnishings. Give more consideration to the floor plan and layout of the kitchen than to the current owner's sense of style.

Make a checklist and rate the various items of each home. Outside, does it appear as though it's been well taken care of? What about the roof and air conditioner? Do they look old or in need of replacement? Look for wood rot around the windows and doors. Is there standing water in the yard? Inside, look at the condition of the walls and flooring. Look for water spots on the ceiling which may indicate a leaky roof or skylight. Consider the size of the kitchen, the age of the appliances, and the condition of the cabinets. Turn on a faucet and check the water pressure. Is there enough closet space? Does the home have a termite bond? Is it in a flood zone? What about the neighborhood, the traffic and the distance from work, schools, and grocery stores?

Take notes and digital photos you can refer to at the end of the day.

Buying a Home "As-Is"

When a home is listed for sale "as-is," it means the seller has priced the home for the condition it's in and is not offering any concessions for repairs. In reality, unless you can pay cash for the home, if it has "issues", your lender may require them to be fixed before granting the loan. Most lenders will require a "clear" pest report, so if there is wood damage or evidence of termites, the problem must be corrected and a clear report issued. When you agree to an as-is contract, you are responsible for any necessary repairs. If the roof is deteriorating, leaking, or has less than 5 years life left, it will probably need to be replaced before you can obtain home insurance. The same holds true for electrical issues and problems with the heating and/or air conditioning. Before purchasing a home as-is, it's advisable to get a home inspection so you have an idea of what costs you may face.

For Sale by Owner (FSBO)

You may think you'll save money by not using a Real Estate Agent, and buying a home that's "For Sale By Owner," also called a FSBO (pronounced *fizz-bo*.) Wrong! Just because the seller isn't paying a real estate fee doesn't mean it will be priced for less. In fact, it may be priced higher than similar homes, because many sellers think their home is somehow worth more than every other home in the neighborhood. Another consideration is that you will be responsible for preparing the offer/contract, negotiations with the seller, scheduling inspections and repairs, and all the other time consuming details. Does this mean you should avoid FSBOs? Not at all! FSBOs are often happy to pay a commission when a Real Estate Agent brings a good offer from a qualified buyer. By asking your Agent to contact the FSBO for you, <u>before you view the home</u>, you may be able to retain his/her services. Your agent can also assess whether or not the asking price is in line with comparable homes.

HUD Homes

When someone with a HUD (Federal Housing and Urban Development) insured mortgage can't make the payments, the lender forecloses on the home. HUD pays off the mortgage and re-sells the house at market value, minus the expected cost of repairs. These homes are sold as-is and offers are accepted during a limited time period. At the end of this period, all offers are opened and the best offer wins. You should have the home inspected to determine what your expenses will be. If you're interested in buying a HUD home, find an Agent with HUD expertise to help with the paperwork and submit the offer for you.

Foreclosures

The foreclosure process starts with a Notice of Default, filed with the Volusia County Clerk of Courts. Savvy investors keep up with public records and will attempt to contact the owners and buy the property before it's foreclosed upon. If you attempt to call a homeowner facing foreclosure, don't be surprised if the phone is disconnected, and if you knock on the door, you may not be welcomed with open arms. On the positive side however, some homeowners are happy to get out from under a foreclosure before their credit is ruined. As with other local real estate, there's a lot of competition for foreclosed properties and they're usually sold long before they're advertised to the public.

New Construction

As mentioned before, a licensed Florida Real Estate Agent can sell any home listed with any company. This often includes new construction in various stages of development. Your Agent can help you find exactly what you're looking for and look out for your best interests.

What Not To Do

Please don't make appointments you don't intend to keep. Not only has your Agent made special arrangements to accompany you, the sellers are usually advised not to be home during showings. This is done for your benefit, so you can discuss the features of the home openly. It's also important to arrive promptly.

If the sellers are home, don't reveal personal information that could affect your ability to negotiate if you later decide to make an offer. It's best to keep your situation and finances private. Try to establish a good rapport with the sellers if possible, and be careful not to make negative comments about the home in their presence. Also, if you love the home and want to make an offer, don't start verbal negotiations with the seller. It's better to put your offer in writing so there's no confusion about what you're asking for.

Don't waste time looking at homes that are way above your price range. Limit your search to the range you're most comfortable with, or that you've been pre-qualified for. Don't count on making a ridiculously low offer on a home because your chances of success are very low.

If you're interested in new construction, <u>don't visit the developments without your Agent</u>. In order to represent you and be paid for their services, he/she must be with you when you talk to developers and/or look at new homes. If you decide to buy, you'll be glad you have a Realtor® on your side of the table when it comes time to fill out the paperwork. The developers have experienced professionals looking out for their best interests, why shouldn't you?

As mentioned before, most sellers require an appointment and/or sufficient notice before allowing someone to view their home. Please don't call from the driveway and expect to get right in.

Don't forget your checkbook! You can't make an offer without a good faith deposit so be sure to bring your checkbook whenever you're looking at homes.

Don't take your pet house hunting with you! If you must bring it along, please try to avoid taking it into the homes you are viewing.

Ocean Living

Ocean Front
Condos in
Daytona Beach
Shores

Lobby view of
one of
Daytona's many
Condos

Ocean View
from the 10th
floor

Balcony view
looking towards
the Halifax
River

Chapter 4

Make Your Best Offer

Nearly all real estate transactions are based on written contracts. An "offer" presented to a seller becomes a "contract" when both parties are in agreement and sign it. To the seller, one example of a strong offer is one that includes a qualified buyer, full or greater than asking price, conventional financing, a substantial good faith deposit, a sizeable down payment, no contingencies, and a quick closing (or a suitcase full of money). In this chapter I'll discuss how to structure your offer so it's the best it can be for your situation, and how the offering price and contingencies are represented.

Asking vs. Offering price

When you've found the home you want and are ready to make an offer, the first thing you need to ask yourself is "How badly do I want it?" Do you want to take a chance on losing the home to someone else by making a low offer? Don't let emotions influence your decisions, and don't believe that everyone prices their home for more than they'll really take. A lot of research goes into the listing price of a home so it will sell quickly at fair market value.

Consider a $150,000 home loan financed at 6.5% over 30 years. If you offer to pay the full asking price of $150,000, your payment (before taxes and insurance) will be roughly $948 per month. If you make a low offer of $140,000 your payment will be roughly $884, a savings of $64. Do you want to lose the home to another buyer because of $64 per month? This doesn't mean you can't offer less, but a lot depends on the price of the home and how long it's been on the market. If you really want the home, offer **more** than the asking price. If you offer an extra $1,000 ($151,000,) your monthly mortgage payment will be $954, an increase of only $6.00 per month. In fairness I must point out that over the life of a 30 year loan, the difference in cost between a low offer and a higher offer will be significant. Even so, always make your "highest and best offer." Your hope is that the seller will review your offer and sign it quickly. The longer the home is on the market, the more opportunity there is for someone else to submit a better offer. Even when your offer is the first one presented, the seller is under no obligation to negotiate with you or respond to your offer. If you make an offer that's much less than the asking price, the seller can simply ignore it and wait until better offers come in. While you may think it's crazy to offer more than the asking price, in a competitive price range, it's not unusual. The more competition there is, the less room, and time, there is to negotiate.

Contingencies and Time Considerations

Any condition that must be met before you can close on the home is considered a "contingency." To the seller, contingencies offer more potential for the contract to fall apart, and may give you the right to back out of the purchase. A strong offer will have few contingencies, and will attempt to resolve or "clear" them quickly. They must also be clearly spelled out. Time sensitive contingencies include financing, inspections, repairs, appraisal, and the survey. Some sellers may want to move right away and others may need time to find a new home. Either way, sellers don't want to take their home off the market for an extended period of time while you get things done. Plan on taking care of these items as quickly as you can. This will reduce the amount of time the home is off the market if you later need to withdraw your offer.

Inspections

Make your offer contingent on a clean bill of health for the home. If your home inspection reveals major problems, you want the option to rescind your offer and have your good faith deposit returned. It's best to have the inspections performed within 5-7 business days.

Financing

In order to proceed with your purchase, you'll want the offer to be contingent on successful financing at a reasonable interest rate. If you've been pre-qualified, this should not be an issue. Unless you're paying with cash, you must be at least pre-qualified for a seller to even consider your offer, no matter how good it is. If you are making a cash offer, you may be asked to provide a statement from your bank to verify that you have the funds available to purchase the home.

Appraisal

Lenders will not loan more on a home than it's worth, so lenders nearly always require an appraisal. The appraiser will visit the home, take measurements, notes and photographs, then compare it to other recently sold homes in the area. If the home passes appraisal (value of the home is equal to or greater than the sales price), the lender will proceed with financing. While I've discussed financing and appraisal as separate contingencies, they may be thought of as one since the appraisal affects financing.

Home to sell

Do you need to sell the home you live in now before you purchase the new one? If not, that's great. Knowing you can move quickly will make your offer even stronger. If you do have a home to sell, as long as it's appropriately priced, it may not be a concern. A lot depends on the seller's timetable and reason for selling. Sellers may or may not be willing to wait for you to sell your home. In general, an offer contingent on the sale of another home is less desirable than one that's not.

Negotiations

Real estate transactions are negotiated through a series of offers and counteroffers. When an offer is presented, the seller can reject it, accept it as written, or counter back to the buyer with some modifications. If ANY terms in the contract are changed, it cancels the original offer and is not binding until both parties agree on the new terms, and sign or initial the changes. Items most often negotiated include price, closing date, good faith deposit, closing costs and repairs. While price may or may not be negotiable, you may want or need the seller to pay some of your closing costs. Another way to negotiate is to ask for "allowances" (money back to you at closing) for such things as worn carpets or other needed upgrades.

Seller's Disclosure

The seller must, by law, disclose to the buyer any known facts which could affect the value of the property. Examples include obvious things like leaky faucets and less obvious things such as a failing septic system.

Before sitting down to write a formal offer, your Agent will contact the listing Agent and ask for a copy of the Seller's Disclosure. If the seller has inherited the house and never lived in it however, there may not be a disclosure.

Contract for Purchase and Sale

When you have found a home you would like to purchase, you and your Agent will sit down together and prepare an offer. While the offer could be submitted on a napkin, most Realtors® will use a standardized pre-printed contract containing most, if not all, of the following elements.

- **Legal Description**

The legal description and address of the home being purchased.

- **Personal Property**

Be specific about the items you wish to remain as part of the purchase, such as refrigerator, washer and dryer, and window coverings in order to avoid disagreements later on. If there is anything that you specifically want removed from the premises, be specific about that also when preparing your offer. Remember, this is YOUR contract. Make sure you are specific in outlining what you are asking for. Other items you may want, such as furniture and lawn equipment, should be purchased separately since the lender and appraiser are not going to consider these items when determining the value of the home.

- **Purchase Price**

Here, your offering price, good faith deposit, down payment and other elements of financing are explained.

- **Effective Date**

The effective date is the date you and the seller agree in writing, on all the terms contained in the contract or more specifically, the date the last signature is obtained and all items are agreed upon. It starts the clock ticking to complete inspections and proceed with financing. When making an offer, you want to know as quickly as possible if the seller will accept it. The amount of time you allow for acceptance depends on the circumstances, but usually 1-2 days is typical. If the seller lives out of town or out of state, you may have to allow more time. If the seller doesn't sign within the time allowed, you can take back your good faith deposit and look for another home. In practice however, it's not unusual for a seller to accept an offer after the time limit has passed. The contract must then be returned for your approval. Again, for a contract to be binding, ANY changes must be accepted and signed or initialed by both parties.

- **Financing**

Unless you're making a cash offer, you have a limited number of days to apply for your loan and to obtain financing. These dates are important! If financing takes longer than promised and your contract expires, the seller has the right to put the house back on the market and your deposit may be in jeopardy. It's important to realize that the seller does not have to extend your contract. Your purchase should be subject to successfully obtaining complete loan approval within "x" number of days of the effective date. Normally, allowing 5 days to apply for the loan and 30-45 days for complete approval is reasonable.

- **Title Evidence**

Title Evidence is proof the seller actually owns the house you're trying to buy. A title search will reveal any other claims against the property as well. Examples are tax liens, mechanic's liens and foreclosure. Such issues have to be resolved before the property can change hands. If they exist, they can usually be resolved at closing in the form of checks issued to the lien holders from the seller's proceeds. Your lender will need to see this evidence, also called "title work" at least 5 days before closing. Your agent will work to see that the title company provides this information to your lender in a timely manner.

• Closing Date

Before choosing a closing date, consider how long it may take to get loan approval and complete inspections, appraisal, survey, title work, and obtain homeowner's insurance. Allowing 30-45 days is typical. The closing date will also have to be agreeable to the seller. Some sellers feel the sooner you can close the better, others need time to find another home. Everyone's situation is different. I recommend setting a closing date that's no more than 30-45 days from the effective date. If for some reason, a seller wants more or less time, a new closing date can be negotiated. Obviously, your closing date must in line with the time allowed for financing.

• Assignment

This section specifies whether you may transfer or "assign" your obligations under the contract to someone else. Often a seller will not agree to this, but there are exceptions. For example, if your parents live out of state but want to move to Daytona Beach, they might want you to find a home for them. When you do, you can make an offer in your name, and ask that the contract be assignable. If the seller accepts your offer, you can later assign the contract to your parents. This releases you from any further commitments related to the purchase.

• Disclosures

Disclosures inform buyers of financial and health risks related to the property. Disclosures include special assessments (taxes) levied by local governments for roads and other public projects, health risks from mold, radon gas, and lead-based paint, an energy efficiency rating, compliance with FIRPTA (when a foreign person is the seller), and a property tax disclosure summary. Because most of us are not public health experts, health related disclosures are often provided in the form of pre-printed brochures. The idea is to inform you of possible risks and give you the right to inspect for them if desired. Special assessments and taxes however should be known and disclosed by the seller. Special assessments are charges usually related to public works projects such as the paving of a dirt road, but may also be levied to pay for un-budgeted repairs to Condominiums, Townhomes, and Condotels. The cost is shared by the affected homeowners, and is usually paid over several years. If an assessment does exist, have it paid in full at closing or continue the responsibility yourself. Remember also, the property taxes will probably go up after you buy the home, especially if the current homeowner has lived in it for several years and is enjoying the homestead exemption.

•   Repair Costs

There is a separate clause in the contract that addresses repair costs and who will be responsible for them, in the event the inspections reveal problems with the home. For example, if an inspector finds live termites or termite damage, you may want the option of canceling the contract. Other repairs that result from inspections should also be addressed. Discuss repair costs with your agent. You may want to ask the seller to cover "up to" a certain amount of the repairs as part of your offer, especially if you feel the home may have some issues. It is important to understand the "repairs section" of the contract. Your agent can assist you with this.

•   Attachments to the Contract

Other documents may be needed to complete the contract. Examples of these include:

- Condominium Documents
- VA/FHA
- Homeowners Association
- Lead-based Paint
- Coastal Construction Control
- Insulation
- "As-Is" Riders
- Other

Condo and Homeowners Association documents contain by-laws, rules and regulations, and other responsibilities the new owner will have to comply with. In the case of condominiums, you have 3 days after receipt of these documents to either accept or reject the rules and restrictions. When purchasing a home in a community with a Homeowner's Association, it's wise to write your offer subject to your approval of the by-laws, rules and restrictions.

- **Survey**

Problems such as encroachments, zoning violations, access to public roads, and other issues are treated like title defects and can affect financing. Your lender will expect a survey free of these issues.

- **Liens**

Construction liens can be placed against a property without the owner's knowledge. Further, contractors have up to 90 days in which file a lien once the work is complete. If your seller has made recent repairs or improvements to the home, ask for proof the contractor has been paid.

- **Time**

When allowing time for inspections, it's best to write the term "business days" into the contract so there is no confusion on this point.

- **Maintenance**

While waiting for closing day, the seller must continue to properly maintain the home. The seller must provide access for inspections, repairs, and appraisal, and allow the buyers to do a "walk-through" of the property prior to closing.

What Not To Do

When your offer has been presented and accepted, the sellers are counting on the closing date specified in your purchase contract. They may need the money from the sale of their home to close on a home they're buying. They'll also be making arrangements for a moving company, coordinating with utility companies, and managing many other details. If you don't follow through with your obligations and delay the closing, it upsets the plans of dozens of people and can result in you breaking the terms of your contract. If that happens, the sellers have no obligation to continue working with you, and may not be willing to release your good faith deposit. If something that could affect the closing date does come up, keep your Agent informed so a small issue doesn't become a big one.

Local Favorites

The Ocean
Deck
Restaurant/Bar

Franks
Front Row
(live music)

**Salty Dog
Surf Shop**

**Maui Nix
Surf Shop**

Views of Ormond Beach

Boy Scout dock
on the Halifax
River

Ormond Beach
City Hall

Ormond Heritage condos on the Halifax River

Site of future home development in Ormond Beach

Chapter 5

What's Next?

In this section, I discuss the steps taken once your offer is accepted, and some of the things that can go wrong. Remember that once an offer is accepted and signed by both parties, it becomes a **binding contract**. This means you are responsible for knowing what you have agreed to, and that you are bound to follow through as promised.

Loan Approval

Loan approval is the process of getting fully qualified for a loan. Expect to be asked to provide tax returns, pay stubs, bank statements, and payoff balances on loans and credit cards. The lender will look at your income, financial obligations, checking and savings account balances, and do a credit check. Based on this information, the lender will be able to give you a loan amount, and a solid commitment on a loan. You'll also know approximately how much money you'll need up front, and what your monthly mortgage payment will be.

You need to apply for the loan within the time limits set forth in the contract. Don't put this off. The appraisal needs to be ordered as soon as possible, and the title work can't be finished until the lender has your "loan package" completed.

As discussed previously, failure to apply for financing in a timely manner can cause you to lose the home and possibly your good faith deposit. If you can't get loan approval you may not lose your deposit, but you must at least apply for the loan within the time limits set forth in your contract. Always keep your Agent informed of your progress and/or lack of it.

The Home/Pest Inspections

Most buyers, excited about the home they're buying, are hoping the inspectors won't find anything wrong that could affect their purchase. However, if there are problems with the home, you **want** the inspectors to find them. You want to know as much about the home as possible before buying it.

The home inspector will look at the structure and all the major systems. Items inspected include the roof, walls, floors, ceilings, attic, foundation, appliances, and heating/cooling, plumbing, and electrical systems. Plan on attending so you can meet the inspector and ask questions. It's much easier to understand the issues when the inspector is there in person, to explain them. Within a few days, the inspector will return a multi-page report listing everything from missing outlet covers to major problems found. Sometimes the inspector will also include a ball-park estimate of the cost of repairs. It's not as important to worry about the small stuff as any home will have issues if you look hard enough. Do consider the life of the roof however, as it can affect your ability to get insurance and financing.

The pest inspection should be done by a licensed pest control company and while it's commonly called a termite inspection, the inspectors will be looking for more than just termites. Obviously, the inspectors will look for evidence of live termites, previous infestations, and visible damage. Outside, they'll look for wood debris around or under the home, and wood-to-ground contact of the foundation. They'll also look for wood rot common to decks, siding, doors, and window sills. Because of heat, humidity, and afternoon rain showers, wood rot is common. Inspectors can't inspect what they can't see, and they can't take the house apart to look inside the walls so there are no guarantees. Still a "clear" pest report offers a measure of confidence the house won't crumble around you.

The Appraisal

When a home is priced properly, the appraised value will be in line with the selling price. If the appraised value is more than the selling price then you're getting a really good deal and you'll have instant equity on the day you close. However, having an appraisal come back low (value of the home is less than the selling price) is one of the most difficult issues to deal with. If it does happen, the lender may decline your financing. In this case you only have a few options:

- If the house is truly priced properly, you may ask for a reconsideration, making sure the lender is using a local appraiser who is familiar with the area and the current market conditions.
- You may be able to negotiate a lower sales price. Sometimes however, the seller cannot afford to take less.
- Depending on your finances, you can proceed with the purchase by increasing your down payment.
- You can switch to a different lender. If, for example, you're using an Internet-based lender, they may have sent an appraiser from the other side of the state who doesn't know anything about the local market. Using a local lender and appraiser could make all the difference.
- When all else fails, you can look for another home.

The Survey

A survey can turn up all kinds of issues that could slow your progress toward closing. Examples are improvements that violate local ordinances, work done without the proper permits, zoning issues, and encroachments. If, for example, the survey shows the seller has placed a fence on the neighbor's property, the seller may be required to remove it before the property can be sold.

Title Defects

As discussed previously, tax liens and mechanic's liens must be cleared before the property can change hands. If you're buying vacant land, there may be other parties who own mineral rights to the property who will have to release their rights to the property. Any such issues would have to be resolved before you could close.

Insurance

You'll need an insurance policy on your new home, effective on the day of closing. Depending on the age of the home and whether or not it's in a flood zone, this could take some time. The insurance company may send someone to examine the outside and take photographs before issuing a policy. If you are purchasing an older home, the insurer may require a "4-point" inspection report that addresses the roof, electrical, plumbing and heating/cooling systems. This can be supplied by the home inspector for an additional fee. If you don't have an insurance company already, your Agent can give you recommendations.

Consider the Weather

When a hurricane is threatening, insurance companies stop issuing new policies until the threat has passed. The storm threat can also cause title companies, lenders, and others to close their doors temporarily, causing delays.

On the Ocean in Daytona Beach

Sun Splash Park
In Daytona
Beach

More Sun
Splash Park

Swimwear Shop at the Daytona Beach Boardwalk

Main Entrance to the Pier and Boardwalk Area

Chapter 6

Closing on Your Home

Closing is the process of transferring possession of the home from the seller to the buyer. Here, the buyer and seller sign the documents required to complete the transaction and put the mortgage in place. This is the day you've been waiting for. This is the day you become a homeowner!

The HUD-1 Statement

At least one day prior to closing, the title company should provide you with a statement called a "HUD-1". This statement details the charges you're responsible for at closing and should be carefully reviewed. Common mistakes on the HUD-1 may include being charged again for something you've already Paid Outside of Closing (POC), such as the appraisal. Contact your Agent and/or the title company if you have questions. Contact them immediately if you find errors on the statement, especially if you're closing on the following day.

What to bring with you

You must bring a **certified check** to cover your down payment and other charges due. It's advisable to contact the Closing Agent prior to obtaining this check to verify the exact amount needed, just in case there are any last minute changes. **Do not bring a personal check or cash** as neither can be accepted. Also be sure to bring your **driver's license** or other form of legal photo ID.

What to Expect

There are no hard and fast rules about who needs to attend the closing, and there is no requirement to hold the closing at the title company's office. Typically however, the closing takes place at the title company, and the buyer, seller, their Realtors®, and the Title Agent are on-hand. Everyone takes a seat at the table, and the Title Agent distributes the documents and collects the signatures. Closing forms may include many or all of the following:

- Settlement statement
- Promissory note
- Mortgage deed
- Affidavit of Identity
- Owners Title Insurance
- Federal Truth in Lending Disclosure
- Flood Certification
- Compliance Agreement
- Escrow Account Disclosure Statement

The Title Agent will collect your certified check and distribute funds to the seller, the County Finance Department (taxes), the County Clerk of Courts (fees), and all other parties involved. Finally, you will be handed the keys to your new home. Congratulations!

Fun Things to Do

Ocean Walk Shops
on the beach

Daytona USA attrac-
tion near the speed-
way

Jet Skiing in the
Halifax River

Soft landing at
Skydive DeLand

Chapter 7

Wrap-Up

Buying a home doesn't have to be stressful. It can be fun and easy when you're prepared and understand the process. By following the tips and techniques in the previous chapters, you can look forward to a smooth closing with no surprises. Since buying a home is one of the most important purchases you'll ever make, it should also be one of the most rewarding. The more you know, the better your chances of buying a home you'll always be happy with, and that's what you and I both want to happen.

Every book needs a happy ending and this one is no exception. Hopefully you'll call me when you're ready to buy the perfect home, and it will end with you owning the home of your dreams.

Appendix A—Important Phone Numbers

Electricity
Daytona Beach, Florida Power and Light   386-252-1541

Telephone Service
Bellsouth
Residence   888-757-6500
Businesses   866-620-6000

Garbage, Water, Sewer
Daytona Beach   386-258-3130
Daytona Beach Shores   386-322-5009
Holly Hill   386-947-4163
Ormond Beach   386-676-3427
Ponce Inlet   386-322-6713
Port Orange   386-756-5224
South Daytona   386-322-3002

Cable
Brighthouse Networks   386-760-9950

Drivers License Bureau, Daytona Beach   386-238-3141

Tags/Registration, Daytona Beach   386-255-5111

Daytona International Airport   386-248-8030

Volusia County Schools   386-255-6475

Colleges/Universities
Bethune Cookman College   386-255-1401
Daytona Beach Community College   386-255-8131
Embry-Riddle Aeronautical University   386-226-6000
Keiser College   386-274-5060
Stetson University (DeLand)   386-822-7100

Appendix B—Helpful Websites

Local Schools/Colleges
> County Main Site
>> http://www.volusia.k12.fl.us
> Daytona Beach Community College
>> http://www.dbcc.cc.fl.us/
> Embry Riddle Aeronautical University
>> http://www.erau.edu/index.html
> University of Central Florida
>> http://www.regionalcampuses.ucf.edu/
> Bethune Cookman College
>> http://www.bethune.cookman.edu/

Real Estate Information
> Laura Edwards (MLS Access, Current Listings)
>> http://greaterdaytona.com
> Century 21 (Articles, Calculators & More)
>> http://www.century21.com
> Realty Times (News and Advice)
>> http://realtytimes.com

Local Government
> Volusia County Government (all govt departments)
>> http://volusia.org
> Volusia County Property Appraiser (tax information)
>> http://volusia.org/property
> Volusia County Clerk of Courts (public records)
>> http://clerk.org

Media
> Daytona Beach News Journal
>> http://news-journalonline.com
> Orlando Sentinel
>> http://www.orlandosentinel.com/
> WESH Channel 2 (NBC)
>> http://wesh.com
> WFTV Channel 9 (ABC)
>> http://wftv.com
> WKMG Channel 6 (CBS)
>> http://local6.com

Appendix C—Tax Table

MILL-AGE CODE	CITY OR COUNTY AREA	TOTAL MILLAGE
100	County – Westside	21.53650
200	County – Northeast	23.31450
600	County – Southeast	22.66450
660	County – Silver Sands	22.68180
204	Daytona Beach	25.46896
214	Daytona Beach	26.46896
885	Daytona Beach	23.78096
403	Daytona Beach Shores	22.21850
015	Debary	19.11096
012	Deland	22.64120
016	Deltona	20.75350
604	Edgewater	24.24150
205	Flagler Beach	21.38150
203	Holly Hill	22.46152
013	Lake Helen	25.04550
601	New Smyrna Beach	22.54339
603	Oak Hill	26.24140
014	Orange City	21.47856
201	Ormond Beach	22.53466
011	Pierson	23.65454
405	Ponce Inlet	22.75950
402	Port Orange	23.24000
602	Port Orange	22.59000
401	South Daytona	23.92809

Appendix D—Area Golf Courses

Course Name	Address	City
LPGA International	1000 Champions Drive	Daytona Beach
Pelican Bay—North & South	350 Pelican Bay Drive	Daytona Beach
Daytona Beach Golf Club	600 Wilder Blvd.	Daytona Beach
Sugar Mill Country Club	150 Clubhouse Circle	New Smyrna Beach
Creek Course at Hammock Dunes	24 Creek Course Drive	Palm Coast
Ocean Hammock Golf Club	105 16th Road	Palm Coast
Club De Bonmont at Plantation Bay	300 Plantation Bay Drive	Ormond Beach
Indigo Lakes Golf Club	312 Indigo Drive	Daytona Beach
Halifax Plantation Golf Club	3400 Halifax Clubhouse Dr.	Ormond Beach
Pine Lakes Country Club	400 Pine Lakes Parkway	Palm Coast
Grand Haven Golf Club	500 Riverfront Drive	Palm Coast
Victoria Hills Golf Club	300 Spalding Way	DeLand
Matanzas Woods Golf Club	348 Lakeview Blvd.	Palm Coast
Deltona Hills Golf & Country Club	1120 Elkcam Blvd.	Deltona
Spruce Creek Country Club	2025 Southcreek Blvd.	Spruce Creek Fly-In
Golf Club at Cypress Head	6231 Palm Vista St.	Port Orange
River Bend Golf Club	730 Airport Road	Ormond Beach
DeBary Golf Club	300 Plantation Club Dr.	DeBary
Hammock Dunes Country Club	30 Avenue Royale	Palm Coast
Tomoka Oaks Golf & Country Club	20 Tomoka Oaks Blvd.	Ormond Beach

978-0-595-37255-3
0-595-37255-4

www.ingramcontent.com/pod-product-compliance
Lightning Source LLC
Chambersburg PA
CBHW021018180526
45163CB00005B/2011